Creation Creature Features
Turtles

For since the creation of the world God's invisible qualities—His eternal power and divine nature—have been clearly seen, being understood from what has been made, so that people are without excuse.
Romans 1:20

Wasil Science: Creation Creature Feature Series!
Turtles
By Joseph Wasil
Wasil Science, LLC.

From the Wasil Science Creation Creature Feature Series, Volume 37

© Copyright Wasil Science, LLC.

All Rights Reserved. Picture credits: Pixabay.
Holy Bible. New International Version, Zondervan Publishing House, 1984.

No part of this book may be reproduced, scanned or transmitted in any forms, digital, audio, or printed, without the expressed
written consent of the author.

Let's explore God's incredible creation!

~~Millions~~ of years ago...

This is where many science books begin, based on the idea that organisms evolved from nothing.
There is zero evidence scientifically to make such a claim.
We must look outside of nature for origins.
Nothingness can't create anything.
Somebody outside of nature created all things.
This is what we find in Genesis 1:1.
"In the beginning God created the heavens and the earth."

That same Creator, the Lord Almighty, designed the TURTLES!

Check out the amazing turtle!

God created turtles to be an amazing creature uniquely designed for its habitat!

Turtles come in different shapes and sizes!

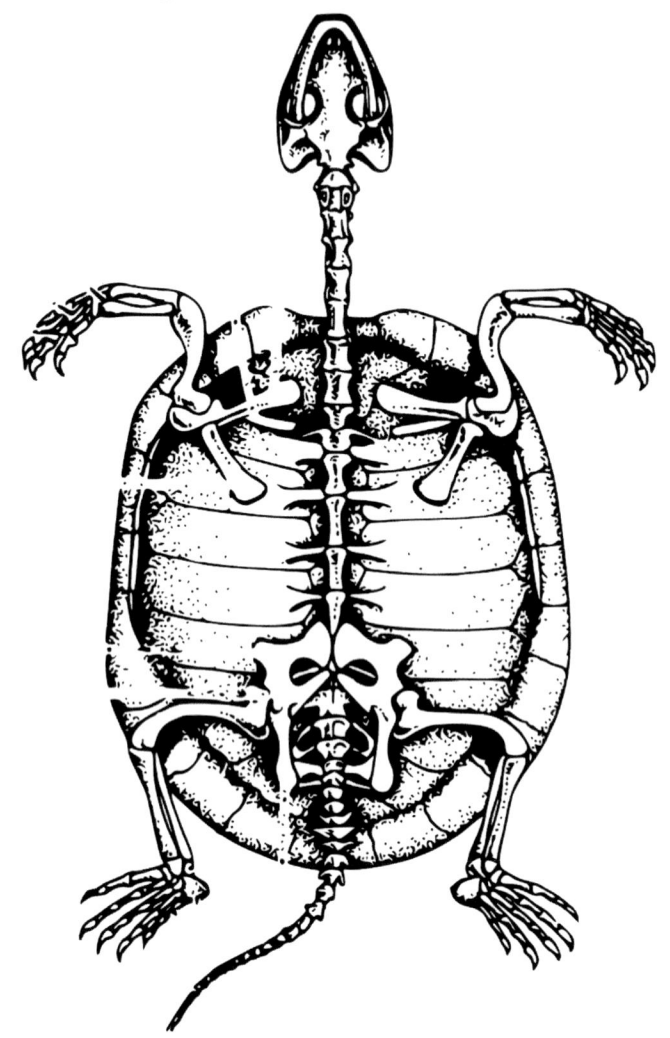

God created most turtles with a bony shell like a shield to protect them from predators.

A turtle's backbone is fused to the top of its shell.

Turtles are their shell which means they cannot come all the way out of their shell.

Turtles are commonly divided three different groups!

SEA TURTLES

LAND TURTLES

SEMI- AQUATIC TURTLES

There are seven different species of sea turtles!

Hawksbill

Loggerhead

Leatherback

Green

...just to name a few!

God designed sea turtles to inhabit almost every ocean basin throughout the world!

Sea turtles often nest on tropical or subtropical beaches.

Tortoises are terrestrial turtles that spend their lives on land!

How can we tell the difference??
FEET and SHELL

Tortoise's feet are designed to be stubby with larger, domed shells.

Turtles that swim are designed by God with webbed flippers and long claws with flatter shells.

Tortoise feet are often compared to elephant feet.

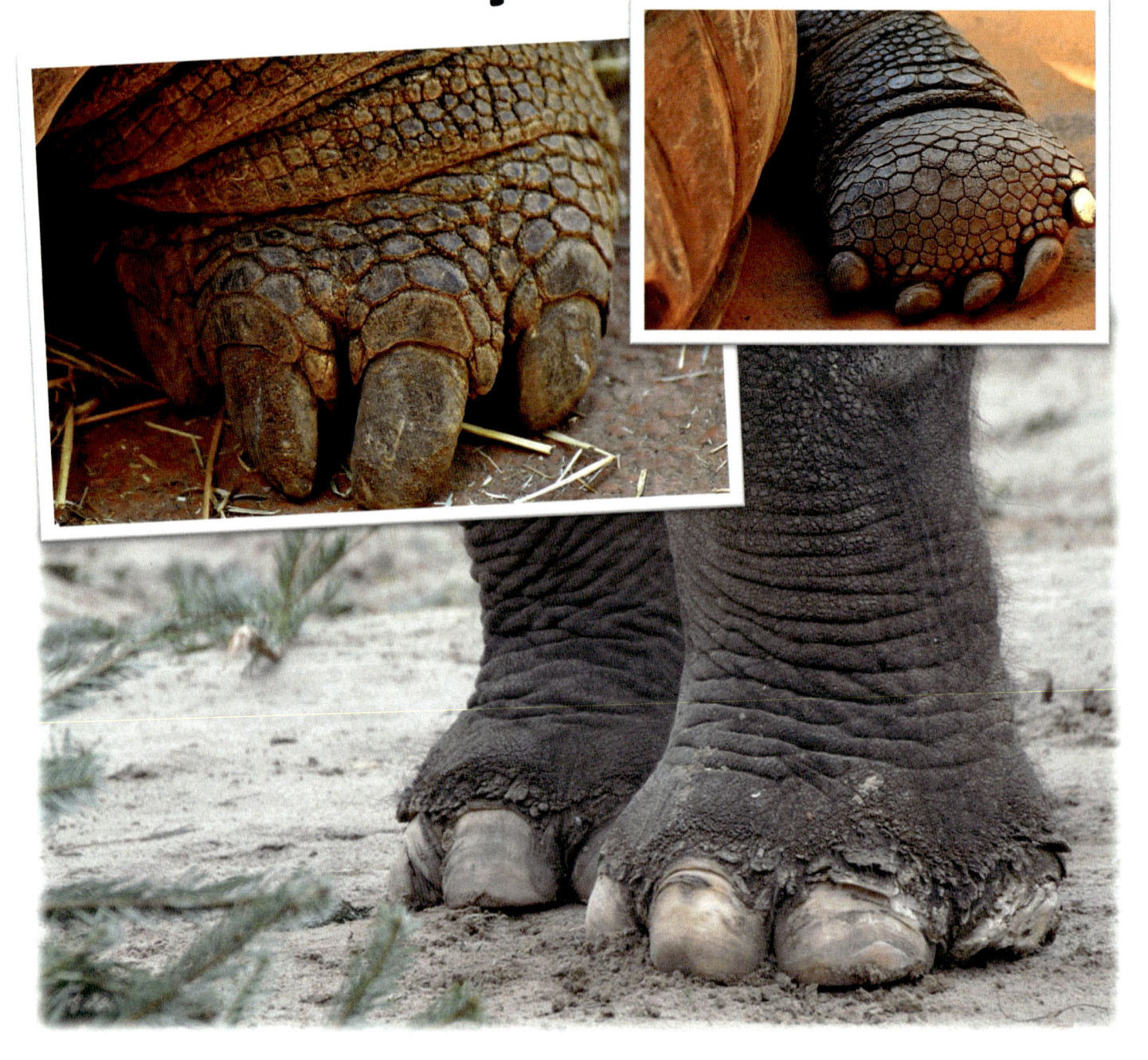

Check out this amazing creation creature feature!

Tortoises are designed with over 60 bones in their shells and each bone is connected to one another!

Tortoises living in hot climates often are designed to have lighter colored shells to reflect light.

Tortoises in cooler climates are designed to produce darker colors which absorb more heat.

Semi-aquatic turtles are designed to spend about half their time on land and half in the water!

Turtles are ectothermic so they must bask in the sun to warm up!

Ectothermic is also called cold-blooded!

What's on the menu for the turtle?

Most are omnivores eating both plants and other animals!

God designed turtles with amazing camouflage and shells for protection!

The upper shell is called the CARAPACE and the lower shell is called the PLASTRON.

Draw and color the different habitats for the different turtles!

Turtles are solitary creatures using their shell and camouflage as the main source of defense against predators.

Taxonomy Classification

Kingdom: Animalia
Phylum: Chordata
Class: Reptilia

Thanks for joining us on this adventure of exploring God's incredible creation! Turtles are an amazing group of organisms designed by God. Each creature has interesting traits that makes them totally unique. From the smallest to the largest, every turtle is created unique by our Lord Jesus!

Made in the USA
Monee, IL
27 January 2025